A New True Book

AUSTRALIA

By D.V. Georges

⊂Φ CHILDRENS PRESS ®

CHICAGO

Reconstruction of the first settlement in Sydney Town, Australia.

Library of Congress Cataloging-in-Publication Data

Georges, D.V.
Australia.

(A New true book)
Includes index.
Summary: Introduces the geographical features of Australia, its animals, and Aborigines.
1. Australia—Description and travel—1981- —Juvenile literature. [1. Australia—Geography]
I. Title.
DU105.2.G46   1986   919.4   86-9587
ISBN 0-516-01290-8

PHOTO CREDITS

© Cameramann International, Ltd.—19 (right), 21, 25 (right), 42 (top left), 42 (top right), 45 (bottom right)

Colour Library International: 15

© Virginia Grimes—27 (left)

Journalism Services:
© Dirk Gallian—41 (right)

Nawrocki Stock Photo: © Paul P. Sipiera—23 (left)

Odyssey Productions, Chicago:
© Robert Frerck—2, 13 (2 photos), 14 (right), 16 (left), 19 (right), 30 (bottom left), 34, 42 (bottom left), 45 (bottom left)

© Charles Seaborn—39 (left)

Photri—11 (left), 12 (left), 30 (top), 35 (left), 40 (left)

R/C Agency: © Earl L. Kubis—18 (right)

Root Resources:
© H. Armstrong Roberts—9 (left)
© A. Foley—36
© Jane P. Downton—27 (right)
© Anthony Mercieca—42 (bottom right)
© Earl L. Kubis—45 (top)
© Maurice B. Rosalsky—16 (right)

Tom Stack & Associates:
© Dave Davidson—11 (right)
© Warren Garst—cover, 12 (right), 29 (2 photos), 33
© Ed Robinson—39 (right)
© Carl Roessler—38, 40 (right)

Valan Photos:
© W. Alexander—25 (left)
© Dr. A. Farquhar—28
© Stephen J. Krasemann—30 (bottom right)

Al Magnus—4, 6, 9 (right), 10, 14 (left), 18 (left), 20, 23 (right), 35 (right), 41 (left)

Cover: Koala and baby

TABLE OF CONTENTS

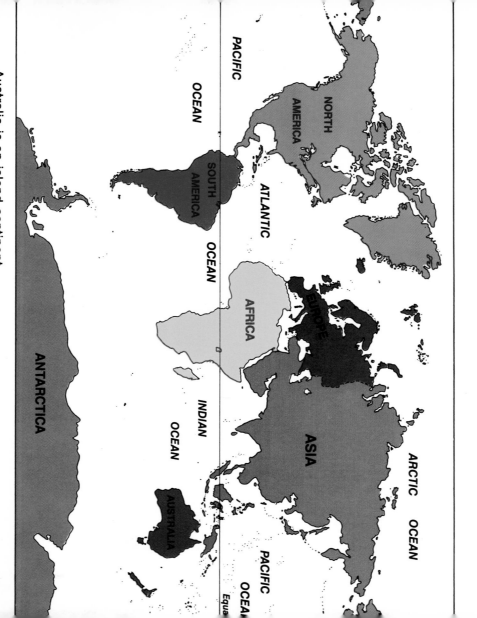

Australia is an island continent.

PACIFIC

OCEAN

NORTH
AMERICA

SOUTH
AMERICA

ATLANTIC

OCEAN

AFRICA

EUROPE

INDIAN

OCEAN

ASIA

ARCTIC OCEAN

PACIFIC

OCEAN

Equa

AUSTRALIA

ANTARCTICA

4

FINDING AUSTRALIA

Continents are the largest masses of land on earth. There are seven continents.

Of the seven, Australia is the smallest. It is the size of mainland United States—not including Alaska and Hawaii.

The other six continents are North America, South America, Europe, Africa, Asia, and Antarctica.

Oceans and seas surround Australia. However, the north coast of Australia is only three hundred miles from the islands of Southeast Asia. And in the northeast, Cape York Peninsula is only one hundred miles from New Guinea.

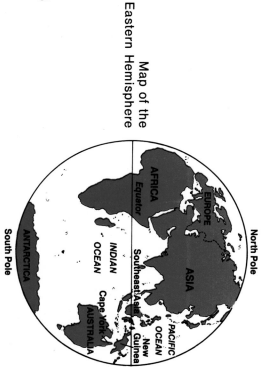

Map of the
Eastern Hemisphere

North Pole

AFRICA

Equator

EUROPE

ASIA

INDIAN
OCEAN

Southeast Asia

Cape York

AUSTRALIA

PACIFIC
OCEAN

New
Guinea

ANTARCTICA

South Pole

A NEW CONTINENT, A NEW COUNTRY

Australia is the only continent that is just one country. Unlike other continents, it has only one main language—English.

In the 1600s, Dutch explorers touched the north, west, and south coasts of Australia. They found dry, flat land. The Dutch called the land

"New Holland," but they did not claim the land for Holland.

The Dutch explorers did not know that the east coast of Australia was different. It had mountains and a rainy climate.

In 1770, Captain James Cook sailed his ship *Endeavour* along the east coast of Australia. He claimed this land for Great Britain and called it New South Wales.

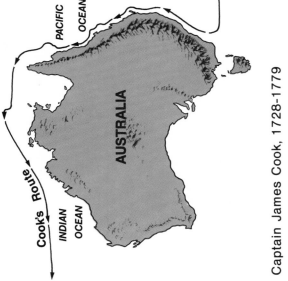

Captain James Cook, 1728-1779

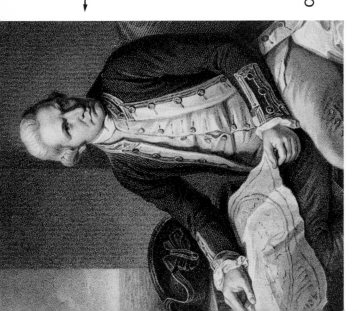

By 1827, Great Britain had claimed all of the continent. It was named Australia, from the Latin word *australis*, which means "southern." Australia's north shores are one thousand miles south of the equator. Thus, the

Map of the Northern and Southern hemispheres

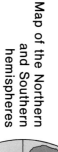

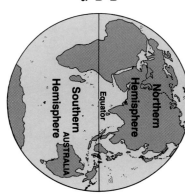

whole continent is in the Southern Hemisphere.

Eventually, thousands of people from Great Britain moved to Australia. But at first, only prisoners were sent there.

Most of the prisoners were sent to southeast and west Australia. They helped build roads and buildings for the newly discovered continent.

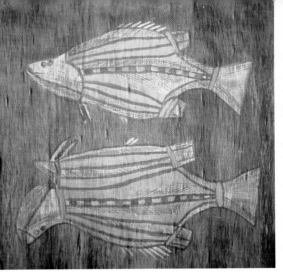

Aborigines (left) make fire without matches. Their bark pictures (right) give us a glimpse of their culture, which, like many other primitive tribes, honored nature.

ABORIGINES

The Aborigines were the original settlers of Australia. They lived in open country, where they hunted with spears. Near the coasts, they caught fish with spears.

Aborigines invented the boomerang. This is a kind of club that Aborigines throw. Because of its shape, the boomerang returns to the thrower.

After the settlers from Great Britain came, many Aborigines were killed.

The Aborigines hunted with boomerangs and spears. It is not uncommon to see an Aboriginal hunter resting while standing on one leg.

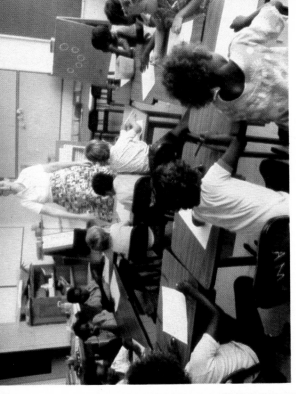

Aborigine school on the York Peninsula

The Aborigines of today live throughout Australia. Some Aborigines, though, live on special reserves. In schools on the reserves, classes are taught in English and Aboriginal languages.

THE GREAT DIVIDING RANGE

The Great Dividing Range is a long mountain chain near the east coast of Australia. It stretches from south of the Cape

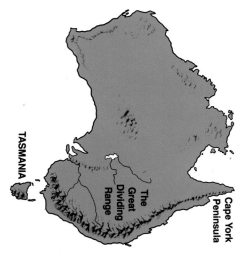

The Great Dividing Range separates the flow of rainwater. Waters that flow down the eastern slopes go to the ocean. Waters that flow down the western slopes of the mountains go to the Central Lowlands.

The waters of Bass Strait, which separate Australia from Tasmania, have carved unusual rock formations.

York Peninsula to the island of Tasmania.

Bass Strait separates Tasmania from Australia. Millions of years ago, a giant valley formed in the Great Dividing Range near Tasmania. Seawater crept into the valley and Tasmania became a separate island.

More rain falls along the Great Dividing Range than in other parts of Australia. Also, the climate is pleasant. Summers are warm and winters are mild.

Because more rain falls, land near the mountains is

Prize winning Merino ram (left). The land near the mountains (below) is good for farming.

better for farming and grazing.

More sheep are raised in Australia than in any other country.

The highest peaks of the Great Dividing Range are in the southeast. They are called the Australian Alps. They are covered with snow half of the year.

In the Australian Alps, Mount Kosciusko rises to 7,310 feet. It is the tallest mountain in Australia.

18

The capital of Australia—
Canberra—is in the
Australian Alps. Canberra
lies fifty miles northeast of
Mount Kosciusko.

Most people of Australia
live near the Great
Dividing Range. The most
important cities are also in
this eastern region.

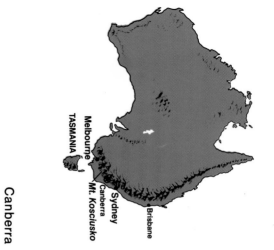

Canberra

Melbourne (left) and Sydney (right) with its unusual opera house

Sydney and Brisbane are large ports on the east coast. Melbourne is a large port in the southeast.

Every day, ships in the ports load wool, wheat, sugar, and fruit from the farms. Australia exports these products to many other countries.

THE GREAT ARTESIAN BASIN

Plains lie to the west of the Great Dividing Range. The climate there is hot and dry. However, rocks far below the surface of the plains have much water in them. These rocks are part of the Great Artesian Basin of Australia.

Artesian water is water that can flow up to the

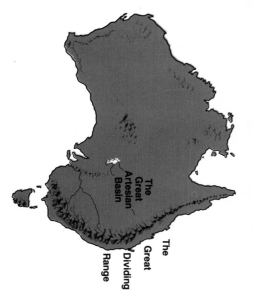

The Great Artesian Basin

The Great Dividing Range

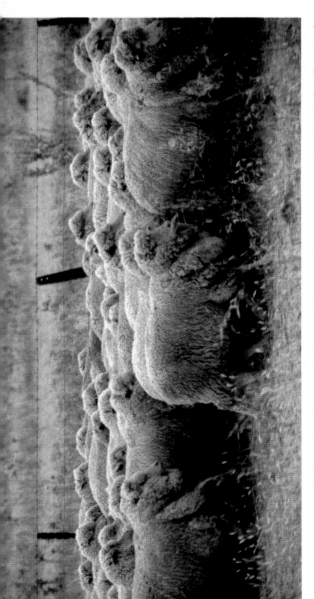

Salty water from artesian wells can, in some cases, be drunk by livestock.

earth's surface from underground.

In some places on the plains, there are natural springs of water. In many other places, water must be pumped from underground. The water in the Great Artesian Basin comes from the rain that falls on the Great Dividing Range. Slowly, the water seeps into the ground and flows westward through underground rocks.

With the help of artesian water, cattle and sheep are raised on the plains of the Great Artesian Basin.

There are artesian basins in many parts of other continents. But the Great Artesian Basin of Australia is the largest in the world.

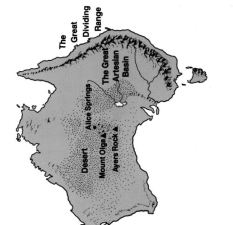

The Great Dividing Range
The Great Artesian Basin
Alice Springs
Desert
Mount Olga ▲
Ayers Rock ▲

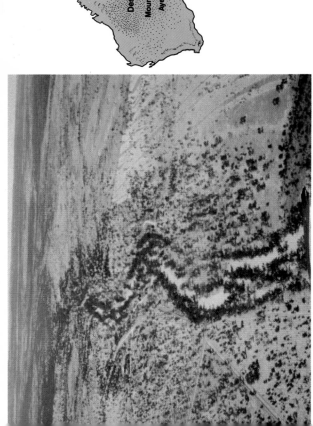

THE OUTBACK

One third of Australia is a desert. Australians call the lonely desert region the outback. In fact, the outback is "out in the back" of the mountains and cities.

The outback begins west of the plains of the Great Artesian Basin. From there, it stretches across the continent to the west coast of Australia. Few people live in the outback.

The climate is usually hot and dry, but some rain falls. Grass and shrubs may grow. Where enough grass grows, cattle and sheep are raised. However, much of the outback is completely sandy and barren.

WARNING
ADELAIDE — 1062
TRAVELLER'S :
CHECK YOUR FOOD, PETROL AND
WATER-THE NEXT PUBLIC STORE
IS KULGERA. 168 MILES SOUTH

Warning sign (left) and the Devil's Marbles, carved after centuries of erosion (right), are vivid reminders that the outback is a harsh and unforgiving land.

Strong desert winds wear away parts of rocks. This process is called erosion. Because of erosion by the wind, desert rocks appear carved. Many rocks in the outback have unusual shapes. Some

26

have shapes like pillars or domes. Rocks with very steep sides are called buttes.

The red center of the outback is famous for the unusual shapes of its red rocks. The red center is near the very center of Australia.

Alice Springs is an important town in the red center. It is on the main highway of the outback. Tourists stay in Alice

Alice Springs (left) and Mount Olga (above)

Springs while sight-seeing. The most spectacular rocks are Ayers Rock, Mount Olga, and Mount Conner. They are in the Ayers Rock-Mount Olga National Park.

Ayers Rock is a single unit over one thousand feet high. Mount Olga is one of thirty huge rock domes. Together the domes are called the Olga Rocks.

Nearby Mount Conner is shaped like a giant horseshoe.

28

Emu (left) is over five feet tall.
The frilled lizard (above) sometimes runs standing up.

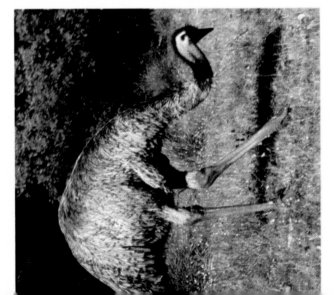

The frilled lizard and emu live in the outback. When the frilled lizard senses trouble, its frill sticks out and scares enemies.

The large emu does not fly, but it can run fast.

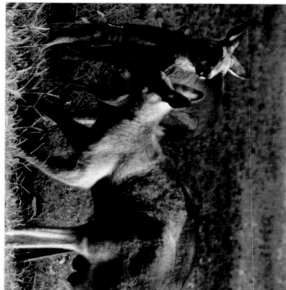

Both gray (right) and red kangaroos (below right) can be a hazard to motorists. Thus, warning signs are posted along the roads.

KANGAROOS, KOALAS, AND WOMBATS

Kangaroos, koalas, and wombats are members of a group of animals called marsupials. Marsupials carry their young in pouches. The only marsupial that does not live in Australia is the opossum.

Kangaroos live in the outback and in the plains

of the Great Artesian Basin. There are many kinds of kangaroos. The largest are the red kangaroo and the gray kangaroo. They are over six feet tall and have very strong hind legs.

In one hop, the red or gray kangaroo can cover twenty-five feet!

Koalas live near the Great Dividing Range of east Australia. They live in eucalyptus trees and eat

Baby koalas stay close to their mothers.

only eucalyptus leaves.
After the young leave the
mother's pouch, they stay
on her back for six more
months.

Another marsupial of
east Australia—the

Wombat

THE GREAT BARRIER REEF

The Great Barrier Reef is in the Coral Sea, off the northeast coast of Australia.

A wide variety of life lives on the Coral Reef.

The Great Barrier Reef is 1,250 miles long. It is the largest coral reef in the world.

Beautifully colored corals and tropical fish attract

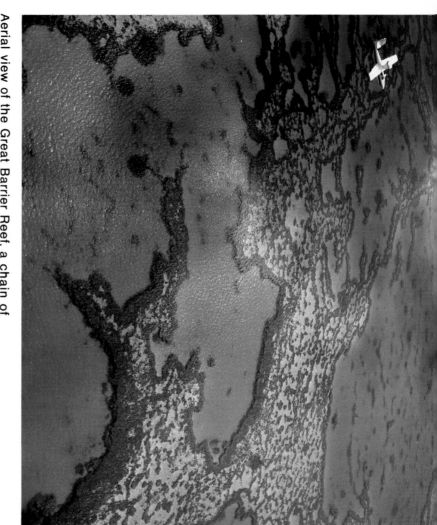

Aerial view of the Great Barrier Reef, a chain of more than 2,500 reefs, that stretches for 1,250 miles.

visitors to the Great Barrier Reef. Corals are small sea animals that live in warm, quiet waters. After corals die, their cup-shaped skeletons remain.

Over time, coral reefs build up from stacks of cup-shaped skeletons. Because there are hundreds of kinds of corals, coral reefs can be many colors.

In the clear waters of
the Coral Sea, coral reefs
can be seen to a depth of
one hundred feet.

Many sea animals live
among the corals. The

Scuba diver explores the more than three hundred different species of coral that live on the Great Barrier Reef.

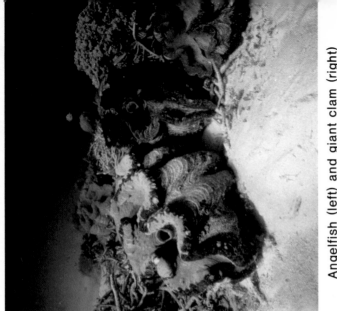

Angelfish (left) and giant clam (right)

giant clams of the Coral
Sea are four feet wide and
weigh two-hundred pounds!
   Angelfish may have
brightly colored stripes.
Some kinds of angelfish
are only a few inches long.
Others are over a foot long.

39

At an underwater observatory on Green Island, tourists can closely observe the sea life and coral reef. Green Island is near the Cape York Peninsula.

40

THE CONTINENT
DOWN UNDER

Because Australia is in the Southern Hemisphere, it is often called the continent down under. It is "down under" the equator.

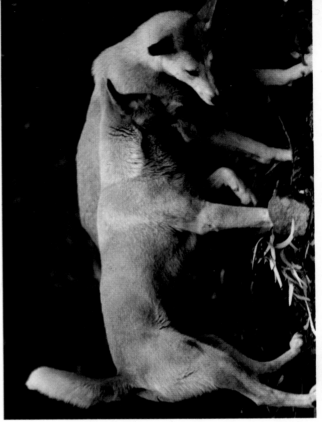

Aborigines brought the type of dog called the dingo to Australia.

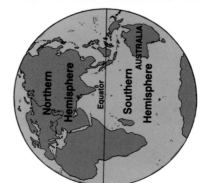

Kookaburra (top left), Manly Beach, Sydney (top right), dairy cattle in the Kangaroo Valley in New South Wales (above left), and a tree kangaroo playing with its young (right)

In many ways, the continent down under is different from continents in the Northern Hemisphere. Seasons are reversed. In Australia, June, July, and August are winter months. Summer occurs in December, January, and February.

No other continent has features as large as the Great Barrier Reef and the Great Artesian Basin.

44

No other continent is home to the kangaroo, emu, and frilled lizard, koala, or wombat. Few places have such a number of strange sea animals living in their waters.

Although much about the continent down under may be unique, Australia is also like many modern countries. Down under, life in the cities is much like life in Europe or the United States.

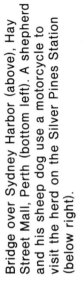

Bridge over Sydney Harbor (above), Hay Street Mall, Perth (bottom left). A shepherd and his sheep dog use a motorcycle to visit the herd on the Silver Pines Station (below right).

WORDS YOU SHOULD KNOW

artesian basin(ar • TEE • zhen BAY • sin)—layers of underground rocks that contain artesian water

artesian water(ar • TEE • zhen WAW • ter)—water that can flow up to the earth's surface from underground

boomerang(BOOM • er • rang)—a specially shaped club that returns to the person throwing it

butte(BYOOT)—a rock that has very steep sides

coral(KOR • il)—a small sea animal whose skeleton is cup-shaped

coral reef(KOR • il REEF)—a reef built up from stacks of coral skeletons

equator(ih • KWAY • ter)—an imaginary geographical line around the middle of the earth

erosion(ee • ROH • zhun)—the wearing down of rocks by wind and water

eucalyptus(yoo • kah • LIP • tuss)—an evergreen tree that has long, dark green leaves

export(EX • port)—to ship a product out for sale in another country

hemisphere(HEM • iss • feer)—one half of the earth

marsupial(mar • SOOP • ee • yell)—an animal that carries its young in a pouch

plains(PLAINZ)—areas of land that are practically flat

reserve(re • ZERV)—land set aside for the native people of a country or continent

strait(STRAIT)—a narrow body of water that joins two larger bodies of water

INDEX

About the author

D.V. Georges is a geophysicist in Houston, Texas. Dr. Georges
attended Rice University, earning a masters degree in chemistry in
1975 and a doctorate in geophysics in 1978.